The Church and World War I

by
Dr Harry Schnitker

All booklets are published thanks to the generous support of the members of the Catholic Truth Society

CATHOLIC TRUTH SOCIETY

PUBLISHERS TO THE HOLY SEE

Contents

All rights reserved. First published 2015 by The Incorporated Catholic Truth Society, 40-46 Harleyford Road London SE11 5AY Tel: 020 7640 0042 Fax: 020 7640 0046. © 2015 The Incorporated Catholic Truth Society.

ISBN 978 1 78469 012 0

Introduction

The First World War has officially become history. The last veterans have died, there are suburbs where there were once battlefields, trenches have become tourist attractions. It is as much in the past as the Battle of Waterloo. Yet in the public mind, particularly in Britain, France, Belgium and in much of Central Europe, it has left an indelible mark. So much seems to have changed because of the Great War: it was the beginning of the end of empires, of European dominance. The essentially upper-middle class and aristocratic culture of the time has evaporated, as has the ethos that underpinned it.

Few would instantly think of the Catholic Church when considering the widespread change that resulted from the First World War. Yet change the Church did, as did its relative influence and power. Oddly, as the following will show, this increased. In that respect, 1914-1918 was a watershed in the history of the modern world, a watershed between the impotent Church of the French Revolutionary epoch and beyond, and the Church of Pius XI, Pius XII, St John XXIII and St John Paul II. The Church of the post-1918 period has been one of extraordinary influence, a true shaper of public opinion; it was the exact opposite before 1914.

The world of 1914 was, in many ways, so very different from that of the early twenty-first century. It was also very similar. There have been a few inventions that have altered the way we do things, such as the computer or the jet engine, but, on the whole, much of how we now do things could already be found then. There was a globalisation process called imperialism, fast communications through telephone and wireless, film, a powerful press, increased democracy, consumerism, materialism and banks.

There was also the siren call of Modernism, which will be explored in great detail below, the call to make new, to alter things revolutionarily. Man was elevated to the centre of things, God was proclaimed dead. At the same time, the old was condemned, without any consideration whether or not change was actually progress, even if it was termed such. The Church struggled with this then as she struggles with it today: *plus ça change, plus c'est la même chose*.

However, and this will sound counter-intuitive to the modern observer, the situation in 1914 was much, much worse than today. As a result of its principled stance during the Great War, as a result of a determined effort to build up Catholic structures in society, and (perhaps most importantly) as the result of the phenomenal success of the missions in much of Europe's former colonies, the modern Church has a much better chance of getting heard than it had in 1914. This book will explore the situation that the Church found herself in when war broke out in 1914 and how St Pope Pius X had understood the underlying cause of the war. It will also examine her reaction to it, how the papacy tried to resolve the conflict and how Pope Benedict XV laid the foundations of the papacy that we see today.

Why? The World of 1914

Ever since the guns fell silent in 1918, the question as to what caused the First World War has been a perennial in the undergraduate diet of history students. All sorts of theories have been advanced, some more credible than others. A.J.P. Taylor argued that it was all down to the trains: once the war timetable had been activated there was no turning back. Others have come up with a sort of domino theory, which suggests that if one party went to war the others, through a complex system of alliances, inevitably followed.

Such determinisms, whilst not without some value, do not get us very far. It is true that the war began over a terrorist attack in Sarajevo, but there was nothing at all inevitable about the political reaction. Europe had often been on the brink in previous decades, but had avoided an all-out conflict since the fall of Napoleon in 1815. The German Emperor, Wilhelm II, made a last-minute attempt to prevent the war, and as late as 9th July, Britain's foreign minister, Sir Edward Grey, could state that "there was no reason for taking a pessimistic view of the situation." He was wrong, for within three weeks Europe was at war.

The factors that contributed to the war have all been chewed over many times: Germany feared encirclement;

Britain feared Germany's navy; France hated the Germans since their defeat against them in 1871 and wanted Alsace and Lorraine back. The Habsburg double monarchy of Austria-Hungary was weak and disunited and feared the aspirations to Slav unity which motivated the Serbs and the assassins in Sarajevo. Italy looked for territorial gains, the Ottoman Empire for survival. Russia's autocracy saw war as a means of shoring up its tottering control.

Sleepwalking into war

The list is long, and all elements were, indeed, contributing factors to the outbreak of war. It could be argued that all *wanted* war and that at the same time all, in the words of Christopher Clark, "sleepwalked into war". The continued debate of the 'why' of the war reflects the fact that no one has been able to explain satisfactorily why every major European power was prepared to risk all in 1914. Reflecting on what had happened, intellectuals in the 1920s and '30s expressed bemusement. This is best summed up by the author Vita Sackville-West who, in Sarajevo in 1936, commented that she "would never understand how it happened."

Oddly for one with such a great sense of the past, Sackville-West seems to have forgotten what had happened in the summer of 1914. Perhaps the sheer horror of it all had obliterated her memory of those hot days that fateful August. Others had longer memories. The great Austrian novelist, Stefan Zweig, recalled the excitement that swept through the cities and towns of almost every European nation: "[T]o be truthful, I must acknowledge that there was a majestic, rapturous, and even seductive something in this first outbreak of the people from which one could escape only with difficulty."

In Modris Eksteins' fine exploration of the mind-set of 1914, *The Rites of Spring*, the historian devotes long passages to this phenomenon. Men *wanted* the war. This is, in part, explained by the fact that few, if any, had a clue about the changes wrought by industrialisation to the process of war. Mass slaughter was made possible only by the advances in production, and by the achievements of engineers and chemists. Few of those cheering when war broke out in London, Berlin, Vienna, St Petersburg or Paris understood that their dreams of chivalric charges on horseback against enemy soldiers in colourful uniforms were just that: dreams.

The realities of machine guns, huge explosive ordinances and, soon, aerial and chemical warfare would obliterate cavalry charges and bright uniforms. It would also obliterate a generation that had gone to their death chanting and waving flags. Eksteins argues that they had not only gone to war, they had actually made that war inevitable. No politician or autocratic ruler could have withstood the public pressure.

European culture in the pre-war years

Support for the war among the intelligentsia was as intense as it was among the wider public. There was a sense that the war would bring about the victory of Modernism, would sweep away the old. In one sense this was true, for the old European order, in place in one form or another since 1815, was indeed swept away. Yet the modernising intellectuals were also interested in the act of destruction itself. There was a great yearning, an irrepressible urge to renew, to cast off what was considered outdated. New was good, old - bad.

This sense of change and rejection of what went before is often attributed to Modernism. There was a sense that old Europe was decadent, that its culture was dying. This expressed itself in a great interest in what was known as 'primitive art', best displayed in the works of Pablo Picasso. He personifies the restlessness of the intellectual world of the time, through his rejection of a single style. Europe was swamped by intellectual 'isms': secessionism, fauvism, expressionism, cubism, futurism, constructivism, Dadaism and surrealism. In music, too, old forms were cast aside, and in theatre, music and dance combined to give us Stravinsky and the *Ballet Russes*.

Underlying this creative fervour that constantly sought the new and which celebrated change, was something rather more disturbing. Nietzsche introduced the world to a thorough nihilism, that rejected any moral or religious principle as devious brakes on natural human urges, as impediments to human freedom. This was not necessarily an atheist view, but rather a humanist one. It did not reject God *per se*, but it did consider God to be a burden on humanity, to be put down as quickly as possible.

Indeed, to Sigmund Freud the ethics which the great faiths traced back to divine injunctions were the root cause of the neurosis of Europeans. His *Civilisation and its Discontents* argued that the great faith-based civilisations of the past had forced people to repress their normal urges, both sexual and in terms of their view of the sanctity of life. Others went further and distorted Charles Darwin's conclusions in the *Origins of Species* to conclude that all life was a survival of the fittest, and that only the fittest human beings deserved to live and prosper. This could, indeed should, be achieved at the expense of the weak, or so Social Darwinists argued.

Pre-war politics and Modernism

In politics, Modernism took many forms. Some, like anarchy, revelled in destruction. Others, like many nationalist movements, became obsessed with Social Darwinism. When translated to the nation, this had profound consequences for a nation would survive only when strong, and how better to express strength than through victory in war? Marxism sought to sweep away old power structures and accounted for the fall of two of the empires following the war: Russia and Germany. Yet all Modernist political movements, whether conservative, Marxist or liberal were based on the same veneration of the state which Pope Pius IX had condemned in his *Syllabus of Errors* of 1864. Pio Nono was explicit: it was un-Catholic to put patriotism above faith.

The Russian intellectual and dissident, Alexander Solzhenitsyn, argued that the 'death of God' as proclaimed by Nietzsche, was responsible for the brutality of the Great War and of the even greater war that followed. George Weigel, in an article in *First Things*, agrees, and believed that what he called the 'spiritual malaise' of pre-1914 Europe was responsible for the war. Both statements fit in well with Eksteins' analysis, but they also suffer from a number of weaknesses.

Religious revival and the response to Modernism

Solzhenitsyn's thesis is the easiest to refute, at least in regard to his native Russia. Czarist Russia was many things, but it was not irreligious. The same is true for the rest of Europe. Intellectuals may have been declaring the death of God, but for many ordinary people he was anything but dead. Religious revivals were normative in many Protestant parts of Europe, and the gathering of the Protestant churches in Edinburgh in 1910 showed how strong their sense of mission was. True, new theological ideas abounded, and many of these shared much of the Modernist agenda, yet that is not the same as a 'spiritual malaise', but rather an issue of questionable theology.

For the Catholic Church this was not a golden age. As we shall see, in many countries she had been under strong attack at various points throughout the past 150 years. However, the great missionary endeavours in Africa and Asia were bringing some tentative fruits, and Modernism was robustly tackled. Whereas political masters and intellectuals either welcomed Modernism or thought it irrelevant, it was only within the Church that Modernism was deemed a sufficiently grave threat to warrant a reaction, and only in the Church that there was a realisation of the consequences of Modernism, even if this prophetic insight was not always expressed in a clear fashion.

Destruction and renewal

By July 1914, the Catholic Church was simply not influential enough to combat the secular expressions of Modernism. The overwhelming urge to destroy and renew, the wish to give birth to a new and, if necessary, terrible beauty, and the Social Darwinist fears of nationalists were all greater than the appeal of the Catholic faith; there were preciously few *catholiques avant tous*. It was not that God had died, merely that he had slipped down the priority list, even of most Catholics. The state, patriotic self-sacrifice and Modernism were all too powerful a pull on men's emotions.

The results were catastrophic. All the urges that Freud and others saw as suppressed by a Christian-inspired morality were given free rein in the chaos of war. Every now and then, the voice of faith and ethics managed to pierce the destructive clamour of renewal and hatred, as, for example, in the famous Christmas truce of 1914. But, although celebrated subsequently, neither faith nor ethics managed to re-impose control over the basic instincts unshackled at that time.

It was only *since* the event, and even more since the horrors of the 1930s and '40s, that the Catholic Church has been able to make herself heard again, this time, more clearly. This was one of the strange and paradoxical results of the great destruction of 1914-1945, and arguably especially of the Great War. The old order, which had been anything but sympathetic towards the Church, was partially swept away. This is not to argue that what came instead was less hostile, but in the world after the Treaty of Versailles, the Catholic Church was rediscovered by an audience that went well beyond those who believed.

The Church on the Eve
of the Great War: France

It is often believed that the *belle époque*, the period before the war, known in the English-speaking world as the Edwardian Age, was one of the Church's golden ages. There was a general interest in the cultural and social organisation of the medieval period, expressed in artistic circles like the Arts and Crafts Movement, and a wider nostalgia for a romanticised medieval past which had allowed even Protestants to create a *Sehnsucht* for a lost era. Men and women tried to recapture that imagined past in their churches, their homes and their lives. This had a profound influence on the way faith was perceived. For many, it equated with aesthetics, and beauty came to be seen as the end result of belief.

The Church had also joined the economic debate. Through the publication of Pope Leo XIII's 1891 encyclical, *Rerum Novarum*, the Church had offered a *via media* in the economic and social perception of the world, neither fully capitalist nor totally Marxist. Person-centred, it had argued from first principle for the dignity of labour and for the freedom of ownership. In many countries, it had a dramatic impact. One Italian commentator described it as follows: *"Leone XIII con l'enciclica Rerum Novarum segnò la Magna charta dell'azione cattolica politico-sociale."* ["With his encyclical *Rerum Novarum*, Pope Leo XIII signed the Magna Carta of Catholic socio-political action."]

Catholic renewal

From this stemmed movements such as Daensism in Flanders, which challenged the political conservatism of the established Catholic Party, *Azione Cattolica* in Italy and beyond, and the attempts by many inside the German Catholic *Deutsche Zentrumspartei* to move the party onto a more social equality platform. This "assumption by the papacy that it had a role in shaping social structures", as one historian called it, was a bold one. It showed a renewed faith in Vatican circles that Catholic thinking had a contribution to make beyond the walls of the Church.

Culturally, in many European countries the period is known as one in which Catholicism flourished. In Britain, the term 'Second Catholic Spring' was coined by Blessed John Henry Newman. In Belgium and the Netherlands, sources of great waves of missionaries, Catholics referred to their time as one of *'Rijk Roomsch Leven'*, or Glorious Roman Life. Great pilgrimage centres like Lourdes rekindled a wider interest in Catholic traditions which had seemed doomed only fifty years earlier. In northern Europe, dioceses were erected in places where the Reformation had swept away organised Catholic life in the sixteenth century.

Yet for all that, the Church faced huge difficulties. In most of Europe, the period between the Franco-Prussian War of 1870-71 and 1914 saw a consolidation of a process of industrialisation and urbanisation that had its roots in Britain. Swathes of people left the countryside and their farms or artisanal occupations and swapped these for tenements and factories. In Germany, for example, whereas 55% of the people worked on farms prior to unification, only one-third remained by 1914.

Population growth and the family

The population of Europe increased from 266 million in 1850 to 447 million in 1910. This put huge strains on a parish system which had been designed to contain a finite number of believers. In addition, growth was uneven. Whereas urban centres like Dublin or Glasgow boomed, rural areas in the Highlands and western Ireland actually declined. Coupled to this was the great wave of migration to the Americas and further afield, which carried with them many priests.

This huge fluctuation in population, and their rapid drift away from the land and into urban centres, had massive implications for the faith. On one level, it destroyed some of the cornerstones of Catholic culture. St Anthony the Hermit, for example, always depicted with his pigs, was far more accessible to a farmer than to a man living on the fifth floor of an urban apartment block.

On a deeper level, the family unit, which in the countryside had meant the extended family, broke down. Children would often work, as well as fathers and mothers, and the work took them away from home. For children fortunate enough to attend school, faith formation was no longer experienced mainly in the organic setting of the home, with a liturgical calendar that reflected life around them in the countryside. Instead, it became something handed down from above by authority figures. In the towns and cities, the ideas of Modernism were far more directly noticeable, as its imagery and language became the language and imagery of advertising (this was the first great age of the advert), plays, literature and popular culture. This is not to say that the Church stood passively by as this happened - far from it. Catholic trade unions, Catholic youth organisations, extensive programmes of new church building and the erection of new parishes and Catholic political and cultural organisations all worked to create a frequently effective alternative to the Modernist message.

Nationhood and nationalism

However, it was in one element of modern life that the Church failed to meet the challenge completely: the elevation of the state as the highest incarnation of all that was good. This was, of course, the great age of the nation state. All over Europe, men and women had helped shape the imagined communities that were the nations of Europe. Many of the countries were new: Germany, Greece, Belgium, Italy, Norway and the Balkan states had all come into being between 1830 and 1914. Even the United Kingdom was fully formed only with the union between Great Britain and Ireland in 1801.

Over large swathes of Europe, nationalities were striving to create their own nations. Poles, Czechs, South Slavs and Irish had all reverted to political and even violent action to gain self-determination. Everywhere immense pressure was applied by the political centre for all its citizens to conform to a centralised national standard. Thus it was forbidden in Britain for school children to speak Welsh or Gaelic, in Germany dialects were to be phased out, and in France people were discouraged to think of themselves as Bretons or Corsicans, but instead to view themselves as French.

Variety was a danger, and the state demanded uniformity. This uniformity cut clean through denominational adherence. Thus, the *Deutsche Zentrumspartei*, which sat in parliament in Germany to defend the rights of Catholics, and which had been formed during the persecution of the Church during the *Kulturkampf*, was deeply hostile to the non-German Poles from Prussia's eastern lands, even though they were fellow Catholics. In the Netherlands and

Britain, Catholics were encouraged to pray for monarchies that, until very recently, had been symbols of Protestant ascendency and into which Catholics were forbidden to marry.

A conflict of identities?

National identity, then, overruled a Catholic identity, just as it overruled local or ethnic identities. In some countries, this seems to be a contradiction. After all, countries like Italy, Spain, Portugal, Belgium and France had a population where the majority counted themselves as Catholics. However, as we shall see, those who governed the state did not necessarily share the faith of the majority, and nor did the Catholic majority form a united block.

It is true that, in a country like Belgium the Church was a powerful national institute. The *Fédération des Cercles catholiques et des Associations conservatrices*, which grew from an earlier Catholic association founded in 1852, grew into the 'natural party of government' under the leadership of Charles Woeste, and it ruled Belgium continuously between 1884 and 1918. However, even in what could be considered one of the most staunchly Catholic countries in Europe, there was a strong liberal current, and many in the French-speaking region of Wallonia had turned to Marxism.

Elsewhere, it was the state itself that had turned away from Catholicism and was frequently even hostile to it.

In some cases, this was because the Church was seen as offering an alternative identity to the state; in others, because elements of the Church had supported a pre-revolutionary regime, and in still others because the regime's own ideology was diametrically opposed to that of the Church.

The most prominent of the so-called Catholic powers of Europe was undoubtedly France. Although badly defeated in the 1870-71 war with Germany, and although slipping well behind the USA, Germany and Britain in all sorts of league tables on economic performance, France was still a formidable power. Her army was the third largest in Europe after Germany's and Russia's, and she maintained a large force of 157,000 men in her vast colonial empire, which included territories in Indo-China, North, West and Central Africa, and smaller possessions in the Americas. Her navy, although substantially smaller than Britain's and Germany's, was still powerful.

For all this projection of force and economic potential, the French Third Republic was a rather unstable entity. It had come into being after the collapse of the empire of Napoleon III in the wake of the defeat by Germany in 1871. However, it was far from universally popular. A sizeable segment of the French population, which was predominantly Catholic, never truly reconciled itself to the Republic, which they regarded as a betrayal of France's sacred mission to protect the Church.

Two Frances

French observers spoke of *les deux France*s, one republican, left-leaning and statist, the other monarchical, conservative and Catholic. The latter group should have been dominant, if the statistics on baptised Catholics are anything to go by, but it was not. For a very large group in France, being Catholic was simply meaningless: one was Catholic because one was baptised, and would want one's children baptised, and possibly wish to be buried by a priest, and that was where matters ended. For this vast group of non-practising Catholics, the fact that the secularist Republican governments wished to push the Church out of the public forum was irrelevant - they simply did not care who, for example, ran the schools,.

Over most of France, attendance at Mass was in the range of between 20-25% of baptised Catholics. And even amongst these there were many, possibly a majority, who did not see the secularist state as inimical to their own experience of faith. It was higher in the peripheral areas, such as Brittany, the border with Belgium and Germany and in the Massif Central, where there was also a residual regionalism at odds with the centralised nationalism of the Republic.

The political defeat of General Georges Boulanger, a monarchist and ardent Catholic, in the polls in 1889 had marked the end of any realistic hopes of a restoration of the old regime, and this inclined even more Catholics to co-operate with the Republic. They were strengthened in their decision by Pope Leo XIII, who in February 1892, advised French Catholics to accept the Republic. There formed an uneasy alliance of right-leaning Republicans and Catholic monarchists, and there developed the so-called *esprit nouveau*, much to the dismay of those pining for the type of Catholic social action that followed *Rerum Novarum* in many neighbouring countries.

From the late 1890s, the infamous Dreyfus affair undermined the *esprit nouveau*, as Catholics attempted to equate the Republic with what they perceived to be anti-French elements such as Jews, Masons and Protestants. Of course, what was being created was not so much a Catholic alternative for the Republic, as a French-conservative-Catholic identity. However, this identity was, first and foremost, French. This becomes clear when one reads remarks by leaders of this movement.

Competing loyalties

Thus, Paul Déroulède, leader of the *Ligue des Patriotes*, could proclaim that he was "a believer. I am a man of no sect, a Christian Republican." Yet he did not wish to see the Church disestablished, as that would have undermined the moral force underpinning *la patrie*. The Church, then, was in the service of the nation. Marcel Habart, another stalwart of the movement, stated that "I am a Catholic but a Gallican Catholic; I am a Catholic in the French fashion, not the Roman." Senior clergy, like the Archbishop of Auch or the Bishop of Nice, subscribed to the views of these men on what Catholicism meant for France. Some religious orders, such as the Assumptionists, also threw their weight behind this type of Catholicism, thereby incidentally incurring the wrath of Rome. Other orders, like the Jesuits, were torn between their loyalty to Rome and to France.

Liberals and socialists began to push for the separation of state and Church around 1900, and soon gained ground. They wished to remove Church control over schools, and thus secure their grip on the young. Just as the French state was removing dialects and languages other than standard French from the country, so the alternative narrative of Catholicism had to go. A concerted effort was made to exclude practising Catholics from government employment, which began in 1902. But it was the government of ex-seminarian and radical anticlerical President Emile Combes that truly went for the jugular. He initiated a full-scale spying campaign that bore hallmarks of later totalitarian regimes, with notes being made of who went to Church, who carried a Missal, who had a cross on the wall of their living room, etc.

When this came to light, the President fell, but his policies to secularise France continued unabated. Between 1901 and 1905, the Church was firstly forced to abandon its schools, and finally was disestablished. A strict law on associations saw the departure of most religious houses and orders. In Rome, the Pope urged French Catholics to resist, but, interestingly, even most of the bishops acquiesced. Resistance was confined to traditional strongholds of the faith like Brittany and the northwest, and soon petered out. Significantly, when the bill was passed in parliament, it was hailed with the shout, *"Vive la Republique!"* The liberals had finally achieved their goal, and the project started by Jules Ferry in 1879 had been brought to conclusion.

The Oldest Daughter of Rome, then, had a deeply unhappy relationship with the Church. Between 1879 and 1914, there was not a single Catholic government minister in a country where 90% of the population were baptised Catholics, and where 25% practised their faith. Oddly, the government of the socialist Aristide Briand made life somewhat easier for the Catholic community, but at the outbreak of the war relations between Church and state were still deeply strained. However, there was certainly a growing rapprochement between state and the officer corps of the army, a veritable bulwark of Catholicism and monarchism in the Republic. In effect, the Republic extended the armed forces and increased its colonial activity in return for an unspoken commitment by the officer corps to the nation. It proved a winning combination in 1914.

The Church on the Eve of the Great War:
The Central Powers

If the situation of the Church in France was deeply uncomfortable, that of the Church in the two Central Powers of Germany and Austria-Hungary was rather different. The situation of the German Church is by far the easiest to understand. The Empire of 1871 was built on Prussian foundations. It included deeply Catholic monarchies, like those of Bavaria and Saxony, but these played second fiddle to the dominant Protestant elements from Prussia. Some 36.5% of the Empire's population was Catholic, and the state of the Church in the various parts of Germany was rather stronger than in France.

Some of the clergy in Germany had been uncomfortable with the outcome of the First Vatican Council, which pronounced the infallibility of the Pope and shaped a much more cohesive and centralised structure of Church governance. Most German Catholics had a strong bond with their faith and in the Catholic states of Germany, such as Bavaria, the clergy saw no reason why one could not be a good Catholic and a strong supporter of the monarchy. After all, it had been a champion of the Church for centuries.

In other parts of the nation, things were rather more complicated. Bismarck, the German Chancellor, had used the minority Catholics of Prussia, including a large cohort of Polish Catholics, as a scapegoat. By targeting the Church, he aimed to unite the secular liberals and Protestant-conservative *Junkers* around his government. This strategy worked. The *Kulturkampf* was initiated in the year of the victory over France and the foundation of the Empire. Catholic priests and religious were expelled, clergy were restricted in what they could say in the pulpit, and, in an echo of what was soon to happen in France, the Church lost control over the teaching in her schools.

Seminaries were closed and Catholic clergy were put under surveillance. Again, there were chilling precursors here to the much worse persecutions that would follow after the Great War. In 1875, the state took over control of marriage. The opposition from the Catholic Church and laity was uniform. The *Deutsche Zentrumspartei*, Germany's Imperial Catholic Party, doubled its seats in the elections of 1874. All of Prussia's bishops and a third of its clergy were either imprisoned or exiled, and the remaining two-thirds were defiant.

Kulturkampf and Catholicism

The resistance in the Polish-speaking parts of Prussia was even more profound. Prussia had gained most of these lands during the partitions of Poland in the late eighteenth century, since when its elite had attempted to Germanise the the lands they had conquered. This pitted predominantly

Protestant German-speakers against predominantly Catholic Poles. Obviously, the *Kulturkampf* impacted significantly on this process. Here, the crackdown was even more severe than in other Catholic parts of Prussia. The Primate of Poland, Archbishop Ledóchowski, was imprisoned. Although Rome came to his assistance and the Pope created him a cardinal, he was still exiled, as were several hundred Polish priests.

The whole thrust of the *Kulturkampf* was that Catholicism was somehow anti-German. Protestant conservatives objected to papal control over German bishops and priests, and liberals resented the Church teaching its world view in German schools. All regarded the Poles as undesirable elements in Germany. Oddly, the whole affair served only to strengthen the Church in the German Empire. However, it is noticeable that the *Deutsche Zentrumspartei* was deeply anti-Polish, and that it became a vociferous pillar of the monarchy: Catholics obviously felt they had to *prove* their German-ness.

The electoral strength of Catholics swayed Bismarck to cease his persecution in 1878. Soon, the fear of Social Democracy and Marxism united Catholics, Protestants and conservatives. However, the rise of moderate Social Democrats attracted many Catholic workers, who felt that their spiritual leaders were too close to the German establishment. And yet, modern social Catholicism was born in Germany. It was a priest from Berlin, Fr Wilhelm Emmanuel von Kettler, who, in 1848, wrote the first serious Catholic treatise on how the Church should react to the immense social changes wrought by industrialisation and urbanisation.

As Archbishop of Mainz from 1850, he published *Die Arbeiterfrage und das Christentum*, in which he relied heavily on the writings of St Thomas Aquinas to describe a Catholic *via media* between capitalism and Marxism. To Leo XIII, Kettler was "our great predecessor" when the pontiff came to write *Rerum Novarum*. Later, Kettler would be the midwife to the Fribourg Union, which brought together bishops from France, Germany and Austria in their concern for social justice. However, the high-level support notwithstanding, Germany's Catholics discovered the same resistance to change that was encountered by their Belgian and French counterparts.

In Germany, there is much evidence that it was only the generation immediately before the Great War which showed serious interest in the social reform question. Whilst a sizeable number of male Catholics joined the Social Democratic movement and turned their backs on the Church, the majority, as well as most of the women, remained loyal to the traditionalists amongst the clergy, and ultra-loyal to the Emperor. This rather odd allegiance to the Hohenzollern, who had been champions of Protestantism and heads of the Reformed Church in Prussia for centuries, is similar to that which may be found amongst English and Dutch Catholics to their monarchy.

The loyalty of German Catholics

In spite of the *Kulturkampf*, then, or perhaps even partly
because of it, German Catholics were deeply attached to
their *Heimat*, be it in the local form, as in Bavaria, or in the
national form. That said, there was a greater attachment
to Rome amongst German Catholics than there was in
France. This combined with a disdainful anti-Catholicism
in the German Imperial establishment. The Kaiser referred
to French and Belgian priests as murderous *Pfaffen*. Chief
of the Naval Cabinet, Admiral Georg Alexander von
Müller, saw the war as a Protestant crusade, something
the Protestant Court Preacher, Goens, agreed with during
a sermon in September 1914. Yet that did not stop the
German Catholic leadership, clerical, aristocratic or
royal, from embracing the war with the same fervour
as their Protestant counterparts. As we shall see, papal
appeals for peace fell on deaf ears amongst Germany's
Catholic population.

The situation in Austria-Hungary was rather more
complex. To begin with, this was not a nation state: it
consisted of an Austrian and a Hungarian monarchy,
united only by the person of the Habsburg monarch. Both
monarchies were, in turn, split on deep-seated ethnic and
confessional lines. There has grown up a tendency amongst
some, particularly of a Catholic and Jewish background, to
regard the old Empire as the cornerstone of 1914 Europe.
If that were the case, maybe it would explain why the old

order collapsed as fast as it did. There can be no doubt that the Habsburg dynasty had frequently been a staunch ally of the papacy. There can also be no doubt that it often was a bitter enemy, too: the troops which plundered Rome in the sixteenth century were those loyal to the Holy Roman Emperor and Spanish King, Charles V.

Conflict between Church and State

More recently, the latest incarnation of the Habsburg ruler, the Emperor-King Franz Joseph, had intervened in the papal election which followed the death of Pope Leo XIII. His emissary vetoed the election of Cardinal Mariano Rampolla, who had been making friendly gestures towards France, and who, above all, had offended the Imperial majesty over his uncompromising stance over the suicide of Franz Joseph's heir, the Archduke Rudolph, at his hunting lodge at Mayerling in 1889. The Cardinal had refused to adhere to the Emperor's request to allow his son to receive a Christian burial, since at the time suicides were considered to be unworthy of a Christian funeral.

The Emperor was furious, and Rampolla had to be passed over. In his stead, St Pius X was elected, whom Franz Joseph held in high regard. Of course, even here the old Emperor was to be disappointed: when the dying Pope was asked to bless the Habsburg war effort against Serbia, the Pope replied that, "I can only pray that God may pardon him. The Emperor should consider himself lucky not to receive the curse of the Vicar of Christ!" The fact that the papacy had signed a concordat with Serbia a few days before the assassination which had effectively removed Habsburg control over the Catholics of the Balkans cannot have helped. The closeness, then, of the ancient Habsburg dynasty and the papacy has been a little overstated at times.

This does not detract from the fact that altar and throne were closely intertwined in the Empire. In 1905, the country had a Roman Catholic population of 31 million, and another 5 million Eastern Rite Catholics, making it the largest Catholic power in Europe. By contrast, there were only 10 million people of other denominations or faiths, including large numbers of Orthodox Christians, Jews and Muslims. However, even here there had been trouble between liberals and the Church, once more over education and marriage. A new school and marriage law passed by the liberal Auersperg government in 1868 had taken most of the Church's powers away, to the dismay of Pope Pius IX.

Church opposition, led by the Bishop of Linz, Franz-Jozef Rudiger, was soon crushed by jailing the protestors. Of course, the move confirmed the almost total control of the monarchy over the Church. Parish priests served as government officials in localities and were paid for their services. Bishops were appointed by the Emperor, and only *approved* by Rome. They were all princes of the Empire, and took their seat in the upper chamber of the Imperial parliament. By 1914, the lower house also saw twenty priest-parliamentarians.

A diverse empire and anticlericalism

At the great feast of Corpus Christi in Vienna, state and Church came together as Imperial troops, the court and the Emperor walked behind the Host, flanked by religious and by priests. Comfortable in his role as the Catholic monarch, Franz Joseph washed the feet of twelve poor men on Maundy Thursday. Famously, when the body of a deceased Emperor was brought to the ancestral crypt of the Capuchin church for burial, permission was sought, citing a litany of all his titles, only for permission to be refused. He had to ask again, or rather, the Grand Master of the Court would ask on his behalf, stating that "he was a man, who begs God's mercy". Poignantly, the Emperor was happy to bow to God, but would not allow the Pope control over the Church in his domains.

Even in the deeply-religious regions of the Empire, such as Tyrol or Slovak-speaking Upper Hungary, it was noted at the time that the vast majority of the congregations were made up of women. There was also a growing tide of working-class discontent, which was stemmed only in part by Catholic social action movements. When the Socialist Austrian Republic was declared in 1920, only 20% of Vienna's population regularly attended Mass. The country, particularly the German-speaking regions, had always been prone to anticlericalism, too, but of a specific Austrian variety. Antagonism was reserved for the aristocratic prelate, whilst the ideal was the humble local priest, who held Josephinist principles of service to the people rather than a life of prayer.

The gradual slipping away of Catholic principles amongst the ostensibly Catholic population of the Empire is illustrated by the more than one million common law marriages that were found all over the country by 1914. These were Catholics who had married outside their own faith. In Vienna, pious women refused to go to confession to a large proportion of the priests whom they suspected of or knew to be living with a concubine.

What complicated matters greatly was the deep level of ethnic tension that characterised the Empire in the final decades of its existence. In Bohemia and Moravia, Czech nationalists bluntly equated Catholicism with Habsburg rule. Many harked back to the days of the Hussite Church, which had been expelled from the Czech lands in the seventeenth century, having for two hundred years been a focus for Czech national sentiment. In the industrial centres of the country, such as Pilzen, many simply turned their back on the Church and embraced Marxism. Yet even Czech Catholic priests came under suspicion after the outbreak of war in 1914, many of them openly supporting the national cause against the Habsburgs.

In Croatia and Slovenia, the matter was very different. There the clergy were usually indigenous Slavs, and in Slovenia at least there were German Catholics. They had joined the Old Catholic Church, which broke with

Rome in 1870 over papal infallibility, rather than submit themselves to a non-German parish priest. In Slovakia, part of the intensely nationalistic Hungarian kingdom, the opposite happened. Led by a Catholic priest named Hlinka, Slovak resistance to Hungarian pressure identified with Catholicism, and, as happened in the Croat and Polish parts of the monarchy, ethnicity and Catholicism merged into one interchangeable identity.

A source of both tension and unity

What is immediately noticeable in all this complexity, is that the Church, usually held to be a unifying element in the Double Monarchy, meant different things to different people, and could be a source of division or ethnic separatism as much as of unity. Leo XIII knew this well, and used missionaries to Slovaks, Poles, Slovenes and Croats as a means of increasing papal control over the Catholic Church of the Empire. It was another reason for Franz Joseph to veto Cardinal Rampolla, Leo's Secretary of State, when he was put forward for the papal tiara.

It has to be noted, finally, that Vienna, and to a lesser extent Budapest, was a centre for the Modernist movement. This was the city of Freud, Egon Schiele and the composers of the Second Viennese School, like Schoenberg, Berg and Webern. They all overthrew, destroyed, and personified the *Zeitgeist* with their urge to create something totally new, even if it was terrible. The city's strong Marxist following was but the political counterpart to this current, as was the surge in a new form of anti-Semitism, personified by its mayor, Karl Lueger. He was the proponent of a German racial nationalism which saw its ethnicity in terms of exclusive Catholicism. Of course, this ran contrary to Catholic teaching; Leo XIII had made it very clear that racism was anti-Catholic when in his first encyclical letter, *Inscrutabili Dei Consilio*, he explicitly referred to *one* human race. He made it clear in a second encyclical, *Quod Apostolici Muneris*, that the Redemption was for the whole human race.

It is ironic, then, that we see in the most Catholic of the belligerents of the First World War, that faith had become a badge of identity for many, something to set them apart from others. One was German-speaking *and* Catholic, as opposed to German-speaking and Protestant; non-Catholic and Czech rather than German and Catholic, etc. Of course, none of this was deeply rooted in Catholic teaching; in fact, it ran counter to pronouncements from every Pope since Pius IX. In practice, the union between the House of Habsburg and the aristocratic leadership of the Austro-Hungarian Church ensured that when war came, it blessed the Imperial-and-Royal arms, something Pope St Pius X had refused to do, but Catholics responded rather differently to the marriage between faith and national identity. Germans, Hungarians and Croats, as well as, initially at least, Poles, happily followed the flag - Czechs, Slovenes and Slovaks did not.

The Church on the Eve
of the Great War: Italy

It is a cliché that Italy is a Catholic country although this did not necessarily hold true for the period just before the Great War. Like Germany, Italy was a relatively new creation. Although there had always been an Italy of the mind, facilitated by the geography of 'the boot', there had not been an Italy as a concrete political reality. One had to go back to the sixth century to find the peninsula under one single political ruler. All during the 1820s, '30s and '40s, revolutionaries had dreamed of uniting Italy under a single flag; occasionally they had fought for it, too, but had failed.

This changed from 1859. The centre of the *Risorgimento*, as the drive to unite Italy was called, lay in Turin, the capital of the Kingdom of Piedmont. Its prime minister, Count Camillo Benso di Cavour, signed an alliance with Napoleon III of France against Austria. The Habsburgs were the main prop of a divided Italy, with Vienna ruling over Lombardy and Venice, and junior Habsburgs in Florence. France would gain some Piedmontese lands around Nice, as well as the ruling dynasty's ancestral lands in Savoy. At this point, interestingly, nobody mentioned the south, or the lands of the papacy in central Italy.

In the first phase of the conflict, Franco-Piedmontese troops conquered Lombardy, and annexed the smaller states of central Italy. This brought the papacy into direct conflict with the now enlarged state of Piedmont, since it lost its north-eastern territories to the new state. Worse, di Cavour was a staunch liberal with a deep-seated dislike of the Church. His modernisation policies sought to exclude the Church from public life. This combined with the notion of nationalist Italians that the papacy, and, therefore, the Church, was the opponent of a united Italy.

Garibaldi and anticlericalism

In the spring of 1860, an independent revolutionary force led by Giuseppe Garibaldi invaded and defeated the southern kingdom of Naples, and sought union between Naples and Piedmont. This left the remainder of the papal states as a wedge between the two nationalist parts of Italy. Ultramontane Catholics from across the world sent volunteers and money to support Pope Pius IX, who threatened to excommunicate anyone trying to annex the papal state. Many volunteers came from Belgium, the Catholic part of the Netherlands and from France, all united in their desire to protect the Pope.

It was, however, in vain. The army of Piedmont, with French collusion, conquered Umbria and left the Pope with a small area around Rome, which Napoleon III forbade the Italians from taking. Six years later, the Italian state managed to gain control over Venice from Austria, which left only Rome. Emboldened by this success, Garibaldi attacked Rome in 1867, only to be defeated by the multinational army of the Pope. Then, in 1870, as Napoleon III was defeated by the Germans, the Italians saw their chance. With the Pope's protector gone, they captured Rome. Pope Pius IX rejected an offer of sovereignty over the Leonine City, viewing it as an endorsement of the loss of his lands. From now on, the papacy became a bitter enemy of the new Italian state, a bitterness increased by that nation's strong liberal-secular instincts.

This also drew upon a much deeper anticlericalism which had marked Italian public life since the Middle Ages. Rooted in the battles between Guelphs and Ghibellines, it had been reinforced by the political power of the papacy and its wars against neighbouring states, by the secular humanism of the Enlightenment, and by the radical atheism of the French Revolutionary epoch.

Catholicism among the people

In the nineteenth century, the liberal-secularism that was thriving in Italy clashed with two forms of Catholicism. One was in the south, where many of the anti-Catholic currents simply had never penetrated. The other was in the rest of the peninsula, where the vibrant resurgence of the faith after 1815 was there for all to see. Catholic organisations, charities, schools and religious orders multiplied. Pilgrimages resumed and strong devotional practices became the norm. The Italy of Garibaldi and di Cavour was also the Italy of St Don Bosco.

For the popes after 1870, the battle with the Italian state was for the control of former papal territory, but it was also for the soul of Italy itself. Soon after Italian unification, the papacy, and perhaps even more strongly, the Catholic press in Italy, demanded that Catholics boycott the new state. It was fine to participate in local politics, but Rome was to be avoided. Although Mass attendance was never particularly high, participation in pilgrimages, processions, Eucharistic adoration and other expressions of 'popular' Catholicism was very strong, particularly amongst the poor. This was true in the countryside and in the mushrooming industrial cities. The Russian anarchist, Mikhail Bakunin, no friend of the Church, said that poor Italians "loved the Church."

However, the parliamentary participation of the poor was marginal, and amongst the well-to-do, the Church was rather less popular. Whereas socialism and Marxism were making significant inroads amongst the urban Italian poor, secular liberalism was the norm amongst other classes. This meant that in practice post-unification Italy was a secular liberal state, with a mass of Catholics who were disenfranchised by class and faith.

After the *Sinistra* of the liberal movement gained power in 1876, the secular identity of the Italian state became enhanced, a process furthered still by the arrival of socialist deputies around 1900. This was strengthened by the monarchy in the figure of King Vittorio Emmanuelle III, who, from the start of his reign in 1900, was open in his disdain for the Church. His governments legalised divorce, prosecuted those who contracted a religious marriage before a secular one, cracked down on pious legacies to the Church and even imprisoned those Catholics who showed support for oppressed peasants.

Italy's place among the Allies

It would, therefore, be very wrong to typify Italy as a Catholic power in the era before the First World War. Even more than France, Italy was a secular country, deeply nationalistic and driven by a desperate urge to modernise without respect for the past. This was summed up in the writings, actions and person of Italy's most prominent poet of the period, the aristocratic Gabriele D'Annunzio. A passionate nationalist, D'Annunzio also embodied the spirit of Modernism through his actions as a soldier and fighter pilot, in his attempt to conquer new territory for Italy almost singlehandedly, and in his embrace of the Nietzschian ideal of the superman.

Immensely popular in pre-1914 Italy and after, the poet-man-of-action was but one manifestation of a distinctly un-Catholic spirit which pervaded Italian public life at the time. The other was the annexation of religious language for the use of the state. Most famous was the phrase 'sacred egoism'. This referred to Italy's policy from late 1914 into 1915 to bargain with both sides of the conflict to see who would offer the best rewards for Italy's support. The very juxtaposition of the words was anathema to Catholics.

Interestingly, the Catholic influence on Italy showed when war broke out in Europe in 1914. Italians were, on the whole, very receptive to papal exhortations to remain neutral, and formed a rather odd alliance with socialists. Except for a few remarkable Frenchmen and Germans, the internationalist socialist movement had splintered over the war, in spite of its declared desire to prevent working class men from killing each other for monarchs and capitalists. Only in Italy did the socialist movement hold out. They and their Catholic allies, the vast majority of Italians, were overruled in 1915 when conservatives, radical liberals, ultra-nationalists, syndicalists and others inspired by the Modernist utopia combined to push through Italy's entry into the war on the side of the Allies.

The Church on the Eve of the Great War: The Other Combatants

The other major combatants of the Great War all had Catholic populations. Some, like Russia, the Ottoman Empire and Britain, had distinct Catholic minorities which were also ethnic minorities and which strove for political emancipation. Others, such as the British Dominions and the USA, had Catholic minorities of various sizes which were, more or less, integrated with the wider population. Only Belgium had a Catholic majority, and only in Belgium was there a Catholic government which was loyal to the papacy and which had the support of most of the population.

Even in Belgium there had been a long conflict between liberals and Catholics, with Marxism and socialism thrown into the mix in the final decades of the nineteenth century. However, the Francophone ruling class and the Flemish majority were both strongly marked by a deep-rooted Catholicism, which was also internationalist, partly because the country was so small. The Catholic Church, both Flemish and Walloon, had received a great boost to its unity through its missionary effort in the vast Congo colony, and through the huge missionary endeavour elsewhere.

It is somewhat facile to say that the Belgians reacted positively to papal appeals for peace in 1914. This was self-evident as the country had declared neutrality anyway and had become involved in the conflict much against its will. The experience of the war served only to enhance the nation's self-identification with the Church. Led by the mercurial Cardinal Désiré Mercier, the Church spearheaded the opposition against German occupation. And although Mercier was an implacable opponent of Flemish claims to more equality, a view the officer corps shared, the frontline soldiers, mainly from Flanders, fought the war in the trenches as if it were a crusade. After 1918, their veteran organisation stood at the core of Flemish emancipation attempts, united under the banner 'All for Flanders, Flanders for Christ'.

Catholicism in Britain and Ireland

If the situation in Belgium was simple, in Britain it was more complicated. There were, in effect, three forms of Catholicism in Britain because there were three separate Church provinces. There was an English Catholicism that was deeply shaped by its past of persecution and which now dearly wished to be regarded as a normal constituency of the British state.

This was accompanied by a Scottish Catholicism that was shaped far more by the experience of Irish migrants to the country, both Catholic and Protestant. Not only were they considered unwelcome by the Presbyterian majority in Scotland, they also faced the traditional animosity of their Protestant countrymen. Most Catholics ended up in the industrial urban complex of Glasgow, in northern Lanarkshire, and, to a lesser extent, in the jute mills of Dundee. There, they imbued a political radicalism that was stoked by their sense of isolation, but this expressed itself not so much in a rejection of the British state, but in a disproportionate activism in the labour movement which sought to change Britain from within.

Finally, there was the Church in Ireland. The story of Catholicism in Ireland is complex, and was made more complex by the presence of two sizeable bodies of Protestants: a group of Anglican aristocratic landowners, and the more prosaic Calvinist working class and farmers of Ulster. These found themselves amongst a much larger portion of Irish Catholics, most of whom felt excluded. However, in the second half of the nineteenth century, Irish Catholics began to organise and press for home rule.

This had been abolished by the union of parliaments of 1800, and now a new Irish nationalism identified the nation with Catholicism. Conversely, Protestants, excluded from this new self-identification, developed a strong sense of unionism. The Orange Order, organised and upheld by Protestant political militants who fought against the Protestant-led United Irishmen uprising of the 1790s, now became the focal point of an alternative, non-

Catholic British nationalism. As the pressure for home
rule caused the British parliament to introduce a bill for
a Dublin parliament, tensions rose and the threat of armed
conflict increased.

The reception of the outbreak of war

For most Irish Catholics, however, there was a sense
that the British state was listening, and when war broke
out in 1914 both Catholics and Protestants served in
large numbers in the British armed forces, even though
the implementation of Home Rule, voted through by
parliament in August 1914, was suspended. There were no
Irish Catholic voices speaking out on behalf of the Pope's
peace efforts. However, fewer men from Ireland enlisted
than from the rest of Britain. Curiously, this was true for
the Catholic nationalists and for Ulster unionists.

For the Catholics in the rest of Britain, the Irish troubles
did have repercussions, particularly as many working class
Catholics in England and Scotland were either Irish or of
Irish descent. That said, there was little if any difference
in the response given by Catholics when the call to arms
came. Again, as in almost every other belligerent country,
papal calls for peace fell on deaf ears.

What was arguably different was the lesser impact that
Modernist thought had had on the country as a whole. For
most in Britain, the war was seen as a necessary defence
of the existing order, a sentiment echoed perhaps only in

the Habsburg Empire, and there only in certain circles. The "urge to destroy and renew", which was present also in Irish nationalism (witness Yeats's description of the violent Easter Rising in Ireland in 1916, "A terrible beauty is born"), was singularly lacking in those going to war. Yes, they went off cheering and waving flags, but rather in a mistaken optimism about what modern war would be like, rather than in the hope that the terrors of war would create something new, something superhuman, as D'Annunzio had believed.

What was true of Catholics in Britain, was also true for the Catholics of the Dominions and the USA. With the noticeable exception of Quebec, Catholics from across the Empire and from the USA enlisted, fought and died on the battlefields of the Great War. Even in Quebec, the reason for this reticence may be found less in the peoples' Catholic faith, and more in a permanent dislike of Anglophone rule.

Finally, in Russia and the Ottoman Empire, the Catholic minorities were despised and distrusted. Poles, Armenians, Ukrainians et al. were totally repressed and disenfranchised. Few suffered the terrible genocide that befell the Armenians, and the Poles managed to gain their independence as first the Russian and then the German empires collapsed. But at the outset of the conflict, and for much of its duration, the Catholic populations of these nations were mere bystanders or victims.

The Papacy and the War: St Pius X

Having thoroughly examined the state of the Church across the major combatants, it is time to turn to the Church's centre: Rome. To be more precise, the Church's centre for this period, was the Vatican palace where the popes considered themselves to be prisoners of a hostile Italian state. We have already alluded frequently to the fact that the papacy desperately tried to prevent the war from breaking out, and that it subsequently was involved in a number of attempts to achieve both ceasefires and permanent peace. What, exactly, was the papacy's role during the Great War?

To begin with, there is nothing like the controversy around the papacy of the First World War as there is around the papacy in the Second World War. This is, oddly, in part a reflection of the much improved status that the Holy See enjoyed after 1918. Simply put, the papacy mattered more to politicians and people precisely because of its role in the Great War. As we shall see, the Bishop of Rome emerged after 1918 with a greatly enhanced reputation, which was furthered by the fact that the Italian state prevented him from attending the disastrous Versailles peace conference, which Pope Benedict XV also condemned as unjust and as a seed for future conflict.

The Throne of St Peter was occupied by two men during the war years: St Pius X, who died on 20 August 1914, and Benedict XV, whose rule extended into the interbellum. Both were united in their abhorrence of the conflict, but played vastly different roles, and not just because Pius died at the start of the war. Pius X was to prove a prophet. He was prophetic not just because he foresaw the terrible damage the war was to inflict upon individuals and societies, but also because alone amongst men before the war, he had grasped the inherent danger of Modernism. Benedict XV was the man of peace, ignored and belittled, accused by both sides of partisanship, exemplary in providing succour to soldiers and civilians alike, and iconic in the way he suffered for his deep understanding of what the war had destroyed.

Prophecies of war

The prophetic voice of St Pius X with regard to the oncoming war has been widely noted. However, it has to be said that he was not alone in predicting war. This was an age of international tension, reflected not just at high governmental level, but in newspapers and popular culture, too. The huge popularity of such works of fiction as Erskine Childers's *The Riddle of the Sands*, or William Le Queux's *The Invasion of 1910*, both in a genre known as invasion literature, reflects that a feeling of foreboding - or excitement - hung over the *belle époque*.

Yet unlike most others, St Pius either knew or discerned that underlying the tension in Europe was something deep and fundamental. What most saw as the causes of conflict - national pride, armaments races, ethnic tensions, economic and colonial completion - Pius realised were expressions of the real cause. He made this very clear from the first days of his pontificate. In his first encyclical, *E supremi*, published on 4th October 1903, he wrote,

> "We were terrified beyond all else by the disastrous state of human society today. For who can fail to see that society is at the present time, more than in any past age, suffering from a terrible and deep-rooted malady which, developing every day and eating into its inmost being, is dragging it to destruction? You understand, Venerable Brethren, what this disease is - apostasy from God, than which in truth nothing is more allied with ruin." (*E supremi* 3)

Now this may sound like a rather typical bemoaning of the 'state of the world', but, as the preceding chapters have shown, there was a deep malaise underlying the cultural and conceptual world of the *belle époque*. Modernism wished to sweep away a world that it saw as rotten, but although Pius agreed with the Modernists that there was something deeply wrong with the world, he did not agree with their remedy.

A changing tide

Many believed at the time, and the myth has persisted, that Pius wished to turn back the tide. He did not. He realised that the dam was burst, but he also knew that instead of coming in, the tide was going out. The civilisation of Europe, its Christian foundations, these were increasingly seen as out of date, no longer suited to the present. It was an odd juxtaposition: Europe, whose nations controlled most of the globe through formal or informal empires, and ascribed that control to a 'civilising mission', actually no longer subscribed fully to that civilisation itself.

Pius knew this, and it is in this context we ought to place St Pius's famous observation to his confessor, Mgr Bressan, whilst visiting Lourdes, "I am sorry for the next Pope. I will not live to see it, but it is, alas, true that the *religio depopulata* is coming very soon." It was a curious phrase to use, but an ancient one which meant that faith itself was to be stripped of people and thus die. St Pius was prescient, but the depopulation had already begun many years before.

There is, however, no doubt that Modernism in all its guises *was* producing extraordinary challenges to the faith. It is to Pius's credit that he understood that, ultimately, this was a more encompassing problem than even the very serious threat of Marxism. Famously, Pius tried to halt the onslaught of Modernism from within the ranks

of the Church through his *Pascendi Dominici Gregis* of
1907, promulgated a mere seven years before the outbreak
of war.

To Pius, Modernism within the Church was a major
factor in the *religio depopulata*. In his encyclical, he does
not mince his words,

> "That We make no delay in this matter is rendered
> necessary especially by the fact that the partisans of
> error are to be sought not only among the Church's
> open enemies; they lie hid, a thing to be deeply
> deplored and feared, in her very bosom and heart...
> We allude, Venerable Brethren, to many who belong to
> the Catholic laity, nay, and this is far more lamentable,
> to the ranks of the priesthood itself, who, feigning a
> love for the Church [but are] thoroughly imbued with
> the poisonous doctrines taught by the enemies of the
> Church." (*Pascendi Dominici Gregis*, 2)

This was a civil war, a battle to close the gate through
which the renewal-through-destruction ideals and the
relativism of the secular Modernism had penetrated.

Catholic Modernism

Catholic Modernism was identical to its secular counterpart.
Both were based on a denial of established values, and both
argued that it was fine and desirable to do away with these.
To Catholic Modernists, the Church was not an absolute,

but a changeable institute, whose dogmas could be altered to suit the needs of the time, rather than express a deeper truth. The existence of religious knowledge was denied, and the intellect and faith were divorced. Instead, what was on offer was a Church that could alter her teachings at will and could discard essentials whenever she wanted.

The similarities with secular Modernism are striking. St Pius X, aware of what the acceptance of such thinking would do to the Church, also became aware of what it could potentially do to European civilisation, and to the humanity of the human race. It gave him a distinct edge over secular thinkers or politicians who wanted to analyse their contemporary society, not least since they mostly embraced Modernism as a 'good thing', one that was 'progressive'.

The Catholic Modernist idea that God cannot be known was not that far removed from the one that God had died; both notions created an autonomous human being, unrestricted by any sense of duty towards the Divine and his creation. Both also argued that the achievements of the past should not be allowed to hinder new developments, and were dispensable. It was not by accident that Pius first applied the word 'Modernist' to the radical reformers within the Church - he explicitly made the link between those within the Church and those within wider society for whom destruction, and the beauty of destruction, was the primary goal.

Pius was aware of the deep-seated desire of so many to destroy in order to create and of the almost pathological need of vast swathes of his contemporaries to get rid of the established. He was, therefore, perhaps amongst the first to understand fully the implications of the assassination of Archduke Ferdinand and his wife by Serb nationalists in Sarajevo. On the night of the deed, he spoke to his powerful Secretary of State, Cardinal Rafael Merry del Val, who was struck by the Pope's haggard appearance. Pius told his right-hand man, "The world war, I know it is almost upon us." Whatever assurance del Val gave the Pope, Pius could not be persuaded that Armageddon had not already been started.

Powerless to stop war

Again one is struck by the prophetic ability that Pius had gained from his understanding of just what Modernism had allowed people to aspire to. He realised that it would only take an excuse for the primitive urges and desires that had been encouraged by so many to become inflamed beyond recall. Of course, the Balkans had been a source of disquiet and conflict for decades, but Pius knew this time it was more serious. He had told the Brazilian ambassador to his court in May that he would avoid a great war in Europe, and specifically said that this would start in the troubled region. He also told him that it would be the people who would force the war upon governments who would doubt its wisdom. Pius was correct on all counts.

At the same time, Pius was deeply aware of his own inability to avert the disaster to come. He knew that the Church's teachings on peace and charity, which he called his "highest ministry", went unheeded because of the demi-god of nationalism and the demotion of God at the expense of the individualistic human being. Both nation and human were told that to achieve their full potential they should sweep away those in their path, and Pius could not prevent this. It was not for lack of trying, and some of the initiatives of the papacy in the decades before the First World War were to bear fruit, but only after the disaster of the First World War, and the even worse trauma of the war which flowed from it.

There is no more poignant a contrast, and no better illustration of how relatively powerless both papacy and Catholicism were in 1914, than that between the nationalist demonstrations sweeping Europe's capitals and the Eucharistic Congress of Lourdes. The congress met in July and was the twenty-fifth of its kind. It meant to show to the world the truth of the Incarnation and the essence of the Eucharist. They were international events that brought the global Church together. At Lourdes, the assembled Catholics sang the great hymn to the Eucharist, *Tantum Ergo*, as the armies of Austria, Russia, Germany and France were mobilising. Whereas Catholics prayed for peace at Lourdes, the secular world, including large numbers of Catholics, were gearing up for war.

For Pius X, the outbreak of the war which he had predicted for so long proved too much. He died 20th August, as the war was gaining momentum. The Russians had invaded Austria, the Germans, France and Belgium, war had begun in the German colonies, and all the main belligerents in the conflict were already involved, except for Italy, the Ottoman Empire and Japan. At this point it still seemed as if the war would be a brief one, and not even Pius X would have been able to foresee the years of stalemate in the trenches, nor the even longer conflict in the East. However, one thing was already very clear: none of the powers, and precious few of the soldiers, were prepared to place their faith above their national allegiance.

The Papacy and the War: Benedict XV

When Benedict XV was elected Pope after a brief conclave on 3rd September 1914, the war was raging across Europe and even beyond. The full horrors of modern warfare were gradually dawning on people, but the initial enthusiastic support for the conflict had remained steady. If anything, the war was now feeding the nationalism of all involved. All this was anathema to the new Pope. Born Giacòmo della Chiesa, he chose the name Benedict upon his accession to the Throne of St Peter. It was a clear reference to the father of monasticism, St Benedict of Nursia, whose motto had been *Pax*.

When Benedict XV published his first encyclical in November, it, too, ran counter to the times. Whereas many in the secular press across Europe were glorifying their own troops and demonising those of the enemy, Benedict stands out for his calm observant eye. He wrote of armies,

"Well provided with the most awful weapons modern military science has devised…they strive to destroy one another with refinements of horror. There is no limit to the measure of ruin and of slaughter; day by day the earth is drenched with newly shed blood and is covered with the bodies of the wounded and of the slain." (*Ad Beatissimi Apostolorum*, 3)

The Pope's focus was individual human suffering. There was nothing on guilt, nothing on glory. What war poets would discover only after years of conflict and bitter personal experience, Benedict XV derived from a Christian-based view of the human person.

The iconic choice of name and the principled stance of the first encyclical would set the tone for the rest of his papacy. However, Benedict had a balancing act to perform. On the one hand, he had to remain steadfast in his defence of the values of the faith, on the other, he had to ensure that he did not alienate sectors of the faithful. This was made more complex by the fact that the Church in individual countries refused to listen to the voice of the Pope; there was widespread nationalistic disobedience.

A protest against conflict

This lack of respect for the authority of Christ's teaching permeates Benedict's first encyclical. He notes the lack of mutual love (which must have been particularly distressing for the Pope to have witnessed amongst Catholics), race hatred (Social Darwinist nationalism), materialism, class conflict and the sidelining of God. These, Benedict made clear, were clear violations of Christ's teachings in the Sermon on the Mount, that classic statement of Christian intent.

There are examples from every country where disrespect for the Pope can be found, even amongst those who served the Church. In Vienna, for example, Cardinal Pfiffl blessed Austro-Hungarian weapons and stated, "We fight for truth and justice, we fight for God and our sacred faith, we fight for our Emperor and our home soil. In this struggle for what is most holy to us, we have God on our side." The American James Cardinal Gibbons, Archbishop of Baltimore, wrote on behalf of all American bishops to President Wilson, "We are all true Americans…Inspired by the holy sentiments of truest patriotic fervour and zeal, we stand ready, to co-operate in every way possible with our President and our national government, to the end that the great and holy cause of liberty may triumph."

Pleas ignored

In Germany, nationalism caused priests and religious to allow themselves to be used for the war effort. Belgian claims of German war crimes were refuted by the *Pax Gesellschaft*. This Fraternity of Peace was anything but peaceful, as their publications in *Der Lügengeist im Volkerkrieg* (*The Spirit of Deceit in the War of the Peoples*) clearly show. And although he had a much better claim to be speaking the truth, Cardinal Mercier of Malines' spirited resistance against the German occupiers of his country of Belgium also began with a nationalist desire, which, as we have seen, also turned him against Flemish claims at home.

In Britain, too, bishops simply ignored the papacy's demands that they support peace. Whereas the Archbishop of Cologne at least prayed for peace, and whereas the Anglican Archbishop of Canterbury actively worked for it, many of Britain's Catholic bishops were so keen to prove their patriotism that they forgot the message of faith and the directives from Rome. The Archbishop of Liverpool, Cardinal Francis Bourne and many other Catholic leaders prayed for outright victory, not for peace. The Cardinal even claimed that it was providence itself that protected the Allies from victory by the enemy; he also rejected Benedict XV's appeals for peace, stating that, "The Pope has proposed that all the belligerents should come to a compromise. No! We demand the total triumph of right over wrong."

The bitterness of nationalism divided even those who were consecrated to serve the Church at the highest levels. When German Cardinal Felix von Hartman suggested to Belgian Cardinal Désiré Mercier that he hoped they would not speak of war during the conclave of 1914, the latter retorted, "I hope we shall not speak of peace." It is rather reassuring to hear that later in the war Cardinal Hartman honoured a request from Cardinal Mercier to treat Belgian and French army chaplains taken prisoner by the Germans as officers. It is astounding, and surely a minor miracle, that the College of Cardinals could agree upon the election of Benedict XV as swiftly as they did.

The Christmas truce

Also startling, in light of the less than enthusiastic response of many Catholics to Pius X's and Benedict XV's appeals for peace, were the events of Christmas 1914. Early in December, in the vain hope that the belligerents could be weaned of their thirst for war, the Pope had asked all to observe a truce during Christmas, asking that, "the guns may fall silent at least upon the night the angels sang." He was ignored by all. However, it would seem that he sowed a seed. From 23rd December to Boxing Day, there were short truces all along the frontline.

Most began when German soldiers put up Christmas trees and sang hymns and carols. Significantly, this appears to have started amongst the Catholics of the 6th Bavarian Reserve Division. It will not do to ascribe all of this to the influence of the Pope. On the Allied side, it was the largely non-Catholic Scottish regiments that were first to respond, and amongst the other participants were Hindu and Muslim soldiers of the British Indian Army.

However, there is no doubt that in many cases there was still a deep influence of the faith on many of the soldiers. In the Vosges mountains, the sound of the church bells pealing for Christmas behind the frontline brought German and French soldiers together to pray. On the IJzer River, Catholic Belgian and German troops exchanged gifts, whilst the Germans promised to take letters to family in occupied lands. Mostly, higher officers, and particularly commanders, opposed this type of fraternisation. On the eastern front, however, high-ranking Austrian and Russian officers came together to organise a longer Christmas truce, taking into account the different calendars used by Catholics and Orthodox Christians.

Although there is no immediate correlation between the appeal for a truce by Benedict XV and what eventually occurred in December 1914, it is clear that his appeal had not entirely fall on deaf ears. It is also clear that faith still meant something that first December of the war. Soon, the bitterness of the conflict, the enormous casualty rates, the use of poison gases and other atrocities ensured that Christmas of 1915, not to mention those of 1916 and 1917, were far less miraculous.

Papal neutrality

Twice during the remainder of the war, Benedict XV would try to create peace; twice he was rejected. To achieve any credibility, the Pope remained strictly neutral during the conflict. This was not particularly difficult to achieve. There was no independent papal state, and the Vatican City state was still in the future. However, neutrality was a stance that pleased no one. To the already deeply anti-clerical and anti-Catholic French government, but also to many of France's clergy, Benedict was *le pape de Boche*, the Pope of the Krauts. We have already noted the distinctly anti-Catholic attitude of the German ruling circles, which was enhanced by the sharp criticism by the papacy of the violation of Belgian neutrality by the Germans, where he was now habitually referred to as *Der Franzoise Papst*, the French Pope. In Britain, even the Catholic press was disinclined to support the papacy over the war.

It would be fair to say that there was an even greater distrust of the papacy amongst the Allies than amongst the Central Powers. At the 1915 secret Treaty of London, the Allies bound themselves to ignore any papal peace initiatives, prompted in part by the Apostolic Exhortation, *To the Peoples Now at War and to Their Rulers*, which sought to bring peace without revenge or restitution. Anticlerical and liberal France and Italy, Orthodox Russia and Protestant-liberal Britain found no difficulty in dismissing the Pope.

Distrust of the papacy's motivations ran deep, and extended to high clergy from belligerent countries. In 1915, Cardinal Mercier refused outright to become a conduit between the papacy and the Belgian government in exile. In France, the same reaction came from the head of the *Institute Catholique de France*. When the papacy resumed its peace initiative in 1917, the reaction from leading clergy was similar. Archbishop Bonzano, the Apostolic Delegate to the USA, had asked Cardinal Gibbons, Archbishop of Baltimore, to intercede with the American government in 1917, to support Benedict XV's peace initiative of that year. It transpired later that the Cardinal had simply ignored the request!

Peace initiative

The 1917 peace initiative was received with profound hostility in France and Germany. The former had lost too much to consider an honourable peace, the latter felt that with the collapse of Russia victory was within its grasp. Italy, too, was loud in its opposition against the papal initiative, and its press began to call the Pope *Maledetto XV*, the Accursed XV. In Britain and Austria-Hungary, the response was more positive. This is interesting, as both empires had much to lose and little to gain from the war.

The new Habsburg Emperor, Blessed Charles I, was deeply worried about the course of the conflict. By 1917, the Habsburgs were propped up by German arms, whilst sizeable groups of Czechs, Poles, Serbs, Romanians and others had taken up arms against their ruler. The Emperor, aware that both his family's position and the unity of Central Europe were at stake, even told Benedict XV that he was prepared to sign a separate peace treaty. However, when news of this leaked out, he denied the offer and his Empire became even more tightly bound to Germany.

In Britain, the conservative press rejected the offer out of hand. It was an attitude which was, as we have seen, shared by many leading Catholics. Oddly, the Pope received much support from Britain's socialists and liberals, not groups normally associated with support for Catholic initiatives. In parliament in Westminster, as, incidentally, in the Italian parliament, opposition MPs constantly questioned their government why the papal initiative was being ignored, but ignored it remained. Once the American President, Woodrow Wilson, widely regarded as the moral voice of the Allied camp, rejected the plea, it quietly faded away. Wilson's remark on the Pope's intervention was informative, by the way, "What does he want to butt in for?"

With it faded away Europe's last chance to save something of the old order. Wilson's fourteen points, rooted firmly in ethnic national sentiment, and the subsequent revanchist mode of the victors at the Peace Conference at Versailles, crushed any expectation that there would be peace in men's hearts. Benedict XV undertook a two-year offensive to persuade all to embrace a peace without guilt or retribution, a genuine Catholic peace. It was in vain.

The end of the war

The Pope's first reaction to the end of the conflict was his encyclical, *Quod Iam Diu*, issued on 1st December 1918, only a couple of weeks after the armistice of 11th November. His clarion call for true peace rings out from the pages of the encyclical:

"...there is no doubt that Catholics, for whom the support of order and civil progress is a duty of conscience, must invoke Divine assistance… Therefore, Venerable Brothers, in order that there may come from the Congress shortly to be held that great gift of heaven, true peace founded on the Christian principles of justice, that enlightenment from the Heavenly Father may descend on them, it shall be your care to order public prayers in each parish of your dioceses in the way you may think most convenient." (*Quod Iam Diu*, 2)

The papacy was not invited to attend the Versailles peace conference. There were several reasons for this. To begin with, as a neutral power, there was no reason to invite the papacy. The Italians and other secularists, too, wished to keep the Pope at a distance, the former in particular fearing that the restoration of the papal states might be put on the agenda. For many countries, the papacy was simply an irrelevance. The Pope was bitterly disappointed by the Peace of Versailles.

Hindsight shows just how prescient Benedict was. He argued that the harsh repayment conditions imposed on Germany would incite new conflict and that the break-up of the Austro-Hungarian Empire would leave Central Europe disastrously fragmented and open to aggression from a larger power. Both were prophetic statements, as was the following, which appeared in the *L'Osservatore Romano*, "the voice of imperialism, hegemonic ambitions, commercial egotism and the overpowering nationalism of the winners" had dominated, while "the voice of humanity remained weak and fell on deaf ears." Some of the results, as for example, the carve-up of the Middle East, are still with us today.

Ironically, the voice of the Pope, so completely ignored during the Great War and its aftermath, gained substantially from its principled stance. As the realities of war hit home, as the shock of the horrors of war turned into aversion, and as the political establishment of much of Europe crashed to earth, men began to recall what St Pius X and Benedict XV had talked about. Symbolically, there is a stark difference between the monument of Benedict XV in Rome, kneeling at the foot of a dying soldier which describes the war as "a useless massacre", and the many that sprang up throughout the victorious nations that proclaimed the glory of dying for the nation.

The realisation that the papacy had been right gave it new prestige. To this was added Benedict's strong intervention with the Germans, Habsburgs and the Ottomans to halt the Armenian genocide, which became one of the horrors to emerge from the 1914-1918 conflict. From 1919, country after country began to establish diplomatic relations with the Vatican, laying the foundations for its contemporary global influence.

Direct Action

For modern Catholics the story of the Church during the Great War makes for depressing reading. In Rome, the Church was led by two visionary men whose voices were ignored by almost all, including by the majority of Catholics and many clergy. However, there is a silver lining. Throughout the war, the Church, as well as individual lay Catholics and clergy, was involved in a massive relief effort. There were also many acts of individual compassion and Catholic love.

We have already noted the Christmas truce of 1914, but the stories of goodwill and compassion are legion. We can start with the papacy itself. Benedict XV did more than try to halt the conflict and appeal for a just peace. The relief effort initiated by the Vatican was enormous. Over the course of the conflict, it spent no less than 82 million lira, the equivalent of £5.1 billion. Its finances were in a poor state, but somehow Benedict managed to get his hands on the necessary money.

Much of it was spent on ensuring the well-being of prisoners of war. Nuncios, bishops and priests visited the POW camps, and ensured that contact was established with desperately worried families. Some twenty-nine thousand POWs from both sides were brought to

Switzerland through the intervention of the Church, where they could recuperate from respiratory diseases and from gas poisoning.

In France, Benedict led an initiative that evacuated civilians from the front to safety in southern France. In Belgium, the Pope, with the generous assistance of the Church in the USA, initiated an extensive programme to feed starving children. By the end of the war, this also benefited children in Lithuania, Poland, Russia, the Balkans and the Middle East. Through this social action, the Church, so divided along nationalist lines, managed to overcome local prejudice and extend the hand of friendship and love. The Pope continued his efforts well beyond the armistice.

Many priests and religious sisters shared in the common suffering of all soldiers. In Belgium, priests were killed by the German army, who regarded them, rightly, as pillars of the local communities and potential focal points for resistance. Interestingly, when Bavarian regiments stationed in Brussels witnessed such attacks, they forcefully intervened on behalf of the priests. In France, priests were called up to fight, and eighty-seven of them received the *Legion d'Honneur*. Religious sisters served in field hospitals, frequently within reach of enemy artillery fire.

Acts of piety and charity

In the trenches, the old secularist mind-set evaporated for all but the most convinced atheists. The stories of men in deep prayer, of rosaries clasped in the hands of the dying, of visions of angels and Our Lady and of miraculous survivals abound. In death, too, Catholicism could overcome the hatred of war. There is the touching story of local French villagers laying wreaths of flowers on the graves of dead German soldiers, with the inscription "Offered by the women of France to the German soldiers, our brothers in Jesus Christ."

Such acts of charity were not confined to civilians. Chaplains on all sides gave the Last Rites to the dying of all sides. Particularly on All Souls' Day it was common for the dead of both sides of the conflict to be remembered at Mass. Scores of Allied POWs reported how their lives were made bearable by the actions of German army chaplains, who visited them and said Mass in the POW camps. Unfortunately, it has to be said that there was strong resistance to such acts of Catholic fraternity amongst some of the French clergy.

In all armies, chaplains played a very important role, and many risked their lives for their fellow soldiers. In every army, there were many thousands of priests who served as chaplains. Theirs was a dangerous function for they were often found where men were dying, which was frequently in no-man's land or at the forefront of an attack. Unsurprisingly, many were killed: in the British and Imperial armies, no fewer than 179 padres of all denominations lost their lives.

Chaplains faced many problems, of course. They faced such questions as, "Why does God allow war?" and some were accused of never being there when they were needed. For Catholic priests, the message of peace that Benedict XV never ceased to give voice to was a great help. Yet it also created problems. The small group of Catholic chaplains in the Prussian regiments faced the innate anti-Catholicism of that country, which was not helped by the perception in Berlin that the Pope was anti-German.

The international nature of Catholicism also made it slightly easier for the chaplains to access the implements for the Mass, rosaries and other religious materials. Except for in the Middle Eastern theatre of war, chaplains often had access to local Catholic churches. The strong organisation of the Catholic Church, which mostly managed to transcend the trenches, the prophetic voice of St Pius X and Benedict XV and the strong witness of Catholic chaplains had one final, unexpected result: conversions. Amongst the British army, there were a reported forty thousand conversions, including several Anglican clergy. Elsewhere, Frenchmen, Italians and Germans who had turned their backs on their faith, returned.

Conclusion

What the above makes clear is that there was no single Catholic experience of the Great War. Instead, the war began with a Catholic Church headed by a prophetic Pope, but divided along national lines. It had been battered by Modernism, both inside and outside the Church, and had found that far more Catholics heeded the voices of war than of peace. Whilst it is true that the Church had undergone something of a revival during the later nineteenth century, it was still suffering long-term consequences from urbanisation, industrialisation and secularism.

The story of the Catholic Church during the First World War is, on the whole, a story that makes depressing reading, nor should this come as a great surprise. If one were to pinpoint a date when the Church reached the nadir of its influence in the modern era, it would be 1914. Unfortunately for humanity, it had not quite reclaimed its moral authority and its voice by 1918, although it was well on its way. The Treaty of Versailles, which Pope Benedict XV rightly denounced, carried the seeds of the even greater drama that was World War Two.

At the same time, the years between 1914 and 1918 severely shook the secular world. Progress was no longer to be assumed, and the trenches proved that a civilisation based on technology was no guarantor of peace and prosperity, but could turn on itself with unimaginably horrible consequences. The terrible beauty that the Modernists had imagined turned out to be anything but beautiful; in reality, it was unbearable.

The prophetic wisdom of St Pius X, the vociferous witness of Pope Benedict XV and the quiet practical witness of chaplains, religious sisters and Catholic laity combined to reclaim for the Church a moral platform within the wider world. In the years that followed, Rome achieved a greater control over local Catholic Churches, and demanded closer conformity with the pronouncements of the Holy Fathers. The threat, first of Communism and then of Fascism and Nazism helped focus the minds of many.

When a new war broke out, the moral imperative of the faith would inspire many Catholics to withstand dictatorship, concentration camps and death. If there were still some for whom the demands of the nation outweighed the demands of the faith as articulated by the Holy Father, there were many more for whom this was no longer the case. The painful lesson of the First World War had been learned by most: the demands of the Gospel are more important than any siren song from the secular world.